SATURDAYS AT THE IMAGINARIUM

SATURDAYS AT THE IMAGINARIUM

POEMS BY

SHAUNA DARLING ROBERTSON

ILLUSTRATED BY JUDE WISDOM

Published by TROIKA

First published 2020

Troika Books Ltd
Well House, Green Lane, Ardleigh CO7 7PD
www.troikabooks.com

A CIP catalogue record for this book
is available from the British Library

ISBN 978-1-912745-12-8

1 3 5 7 9 10 8 6 4 2

Printed in Poland

'You can't depend on your eyes
when your imagination
is out of focus.'
MARK TWAIN

'Everything great that ever
happened in this world happened
first in somebody's imagination.'
ASTRID LINDGREN

For my family

Contents

Welcome to the Imaginarium
(it's not just for Saturdays)

When I was growing up, people would sometimes say, *Y'know your trouble? Too much imagination!* Or, *Quit daydreaming and get real!*

A lot of people seem to think that the imagination is just for children and poets, or inventors and dreamers, that it's something a bit frivolous. In fact, the imagination is an essential function of the human mind and a vital part of what makes us human. Here's what the author Neil Gaiman[*] says about it (I'm quoting Neil here because I couldn't put it better myself):

'Just look around this room... everything you can see, including the walls, was, at some point, imagined. Someone decided it might be easier to sit on a chair than on the ground and imagined the chair... This room and the things in it, and all the other things in this building, in this city, exist because, over and over and over, people imagined things.'

He also says this:

'We all – adults and children, writers and readers – have an obligation to daydream. We have an obligation to imagine.'

An obligation? Wow! As a keen imagination-user, that really got my attention. But then when I spoke to other people about it they often said things like,

Oh that sounds wonderful, but count me out. I don't have much of an imagination. Here's what I imagined myself replying (because, like most people, I usually think of a really good reply long after a conversation has ended): if you're human, then you have a brilliant imagination and you're using it, whether you realise it or not. The question is, what are you using it for?

You see, it's easy to imagine (yes, imagine) that we don't have a good imagination, or that it's impossible to look at things differently, or to change them. But every change that ever happened in the world started out in someone's imagination. Then someone else joined in, and then another, and so on. That's how change happens. It starts with someone just like you imagining how something can be different.

In this book are some poems I made up from my imagination and some artwork that Jude Wisdom made up from hers. They explore different ways of using the imagination. We hope you enjoy them. We'd like to imagine some of them sparking your imagination. We're imagining that happening right now. Here you are in our mind's eye… if we may say so, you look good – really good – when your imagination's all fired up like that.

Shauna Darling Robertson

* In: Neil Gaiman. *The View from the Cheap Seats*. Headline, 2016.

Open Wide

Imagine if swallowing
were real –

if we truly
took things in
through our mouths
and they became part of us.

If my arms were made
of ham and marmalade,

my legs mainly contained
eggs / ketchup / lemonade

and my head was filled with the kind of fresh thinking
you only get from a chunk of chilli-chip ice-cream
slip-sliding on a red hot slice of peppermint pie.

Dear Stars,

We lived among you once.
It was brilliant.

Night never fell
so no need for daylight saving,
LEDs or neon.

Everyone lived on Twinkle Street.
Sunny side up –
all sparkle, no shade.

There was always a glimmer of hope
aglow
eager to grow
to a shimmer,
a beam.

Mistakes
burned up
the minute they were made.

We rose
in the east
and the west

in the north
and the south
and we never went down.

Best thing of all?
My light was always on.

I shone
and I shone
and I shone.

M-M-Murray's
M-M-Mountains

Murray's a mountaineer
who's frightened of heights.

He lies awake nights
getting in frets
over summits and crests,

then scours the news
for tumbles and falls
and for ambulance calls.

He crawls on all fours
and combs the ground over
for lucky-leafed clovers

and st-st-st-stutters
like wind on a tent
before each ascent.

But then, event done
fear flouted, peak won
his valley-wide smile
could outshine the sun.

Uncle Billy is Teaching
Me How to Whistle

We sit on upturned buckets in his herb garden
pulling faces at the parsley.

We foxtrot across to the Friday fish market,
stuff ourselves with sardines,
spit out the spines and scales
and stitch them into superlative silver spacesuits.

Next stop, the corner sweetshop.
We crunch our way
through seven colours of sunshine-scented candy
then rummage for pots of gold
under each other's rainbow-striped tongues.

But how is any of this helping my whistling?

Oh, that, says Uncle Billy.
The whistle will come when the whistle is ready.

So what exactly are we doing here?

Entertaining ourselves while we wait, he says
as he conducts an imaginary orchestra
with a blur of index fingers
that almost trip up a passing dragonfly.

Magic Trick

Dad says
'I don't believe
in things I can't see
or things I can't
hear, smell, taste or touch.'

'What,' I say, 'not even magic?'
'*Especially* magic!' says Dad.

'Interesting,' I say. 'So how about, for example
your kidneys. Do you believe
in your kidneys?'

Dad snorts.
'Of course I believe in my kidneys!'

'Because…?' I say.
'Simple,' says Dad. 'I *know* they exist.'

'Can you see them?' I say.
'Not exactly,' he says.

'Hear them?' I say.
'Don't be daft,' he says.

'Smell them or taste them?' I say.
'Clearly not,' he says.

'Can you feel them or touch them?' I say
and he says

'No, but I remember when I had that scan –
I'm pretty sure the doctor said *he* saw my kidneys,'

and I say, 'That sounds a lot like the time
I told you about the magic *I* saw...'

'That's different,' Dad says.
'How so?' I say and Dad says, 'It just *is*,'
and then he makes a sort of harumpfing noise,
gets up from his chair and stomps out of the room.

I look over at Grandad
who smiles and winks and says
'Magic, eh? Well I see
you just made your Dad disappear.'

Little Brown Cup

There's a cup in the cupboard
that nobody loves.
It's brown and it's chipped
and it's not really big enough
for a decent cup of anything

but whenever someone offers
a hot drink of this or that, I say
'I'll take the brown cup,' and so
they all think it's my favourite cup.
But really, I just feel bad
about the things that nobody loves.

The Nameless

Beneath this river
deeper waters flow.

Inside every mountain
a higher peak quietly rises.

Within each blade of grass
whisper shapes and shades of green

and all the while
a voice closer still

sings of things
with no name.

Before the Birds Took Off

They were everywhere, always under our feet.
You could barely risk a step
without trampling a toucan
or kicking a cuckoo.

And, man, were they moody.
Sweet tweets and cheerful chirps?
Forget it!
Our feathered friends were hacked off
at the lack of space
and getting more feathered, less friendly
by the second.

Bluejays bickered bitterly
about cormorants causing congestion
while robins refused to use the nominated lanes,
grousing they were beak-to-tail
with nine hundred nightingales.

Wrens wrestled for legroom
on the rammed-to-the-rafters railways
and coots cowered, dodging the ducks
pecking at their backs about the transport cuts.

Public parks were thigh-deep in thrushes
while every parrot, peewee, pelican, pigeon
pounded the towns' pavements, day and night.

Something had to give, and it did.
But don't you ever wonder what life might be like
were it us, not the birds, who took flight?

The Followers

ep
heep
heep sheep
p

heep sheep sheep
p sheep sheep sheep sheep
ep sheep sheep sheep
eep

                        sheep sheep sheep sheep
                           sheep sheep sheep sheep sheep
                  sheep sheep sheep sheep
                sheep sheep
                    sheep

sheep sheep sheep sheep sheep
sheep sheep sheep sheep sheep sheep sheep
sheep sheep sheep sheep sheep
sheep sheep

sheep she
sheep sheep sheep she
sheep sheep sh
s

The Dreamcatcher

The old man gave me
this weird looking thing.
A stringy, beady
feathery thing.
A dreamcatcher, he whispered.
Yeah, whatever.
Still, I did as he said,
hung it over my bed

and that very night
I caught my first one
brim-filled
with treasures –
gold, silver, rubies, rings.

Nice and all,
but I'm not what you'd call
huge on jewels
so I held out for another
and sure enough, on night two
I was blessed with adventures -
castles and dragons,
galloping stallions, damsels
in varying degrees of distress.

Come night three, I confess
I was hooked
and from that moment on
I spent most of my days
killing time till day's end
and then sinking to sleep
and waking at dawn to check my net
for a freshly-snared dream.

Six months in, I'm now the proud owner
of five-hundred-and-fifty-eight.
Some creepy, some soothing
some crazy, some straight.

But lately I worry my dreams feel hemmed in,
suspended up there
in my stringy, beady, feathery thing

so I've hatched a plan for their urgent release
and tonight's the night I'll let my dreams fly.

Thing is, I'm thinking I might go with them.
So please keep this quiet.
Goodnight
and goodbye.

Chickens

Grandma tells me
not to count my chickens.

She sounds pretty serious
so I go out to the back yard
and look for some chickens
not to count.

There's no chickens, but luckily
I spot a few ducks down by the pond
and get straight to work
not counting them.

Grandma flings open the kitchen window
and hollers at me not to be so smart
so I quickly stop
not counting the ducks
and pretend that I don't know
what not counting is.

Troubled

I wish
more than anything else in the world
that my grandad
was an octopus.

If I was a wizard
here's what I'd do –
I'd turn my grandad
into an octopus.

An octopus, you see
has three hearts.
My grandad has just the one
and it has heart trouble.

When I Was Cross-Eyed

I thought I saw a loaded fist
                itching for a riot.
But no, it was a tenderness
                resting on a quiet.

I thought I saw a hurricane
                bullying a breeze.
Turns out it was an effortless
                relaxing on an ease.

I thought I saw a naked flame
                flinching from a blow.
Not so, it was a free-for-all
                following the flow.

I thought I saw ten hard-as-nails
                tightening their grip.
Turns out it was a sweetness
                savouring a sip.

I thought I saw a cruel queen
                menacing the masses.
But no, it was my eye doctor
                prescribing me peace glasses.

How to Break the Bad News

Tell them first thing
while they're still half asleep.
Be delicate, gentle –
a whisper, a peep.

Tell them in yellow
so no-one sees red.
Or speak it in tongues
(they won't know what you said).

Keep a safe distance
and tell them by letter.
Slip in a choir –
when sung, it sounds better.

Tell them and offer them
five pounds or ten.
Paying for peace
might just work now and then.

Tell them in winter
as jingle bells ring.
With luck they'll forgive you
by mid-to-late spring.

Tell them on horseback
then ride like the gale.
Or shout it from starboard
and quickly set sail.

Tell them with roses
between your front teeth.
But tell them, just tell them
and feel the relief.

The Poetry Guerrilla

That morning
the world woke up
to poetry.

Like some kind of Santa Claus of words
the poetry guerrilla had laboured all night
spreading the pleasure of line and verse.

At breakfast, the shell from Bettina's boiled egg
unravelled to reveal a ballad.

At the launderette, Susie pulled three pairs of pantoums
from the drier. A little wiggle and they were a perfect fit.

Uncle Jim found a limerick printed on his lottery ticket.
His numbers didn't win, but still, he had a giggle.

Alice the hairdresser's headache was instantly fixed
by a haiku etched into an aspirin.

Reverend Crick, the vicar, found his vestry filled with villanelles
which served as his sermons for the next six months.

When Tammy ordered take-out she got
a triolet with her chicken tikka, spare ribs with a sestina
and a free side order of odes.

But wait – someone had broken into the bank!
(Turns out they took nothing, just deposited sixty sonnets
and a cento.)

Order! cried Captain Collis, as he sought to calm the crowd
with a warning shot from his hilltop cannon.
But it fired cantos, not cannonballs,
littering the town with a lengthy, living legend.

Brushing my teeth at bedtime, I noticed
a fading clerihew finger-written on the foggy bathroom window.
It had my name on it
and as I looked up I swear I saw
a shadowy figure heading for the horizon.
Man? Woman? Child?
I couldn't say, but this I know –

there was a spring in their step,
a glint in their eye
and so much language on their lips.

Earthtalk

The sea has a story to tell us
>   if only we'd wait on the beach.

And I wish we'd just sit here and listen
>   to all that the wind has to teach.

The earth will share mountains of wisdom
>   as soon as we grasp more than speech.

The trees gently whisper their secrets
>   and offer up knowledge for free.

The birds chatter openly to us –
>   *whatever seems locked, there's a key.*

The whole world, it talks to us daily.
>   Can't anyone hear it but me?

Liwuli for Venus
(Where a Day Lasts Longer Than a Year)

Orbit the sun while spinning on your axis. Don't give
time a second thought. Forget trying hard, just let loose.
Give it all you've got …

Look at you go –
fearless and free!
A warm wind in your sails.

Who cares if your days are long,
your years short?

A day really does last longer than a year on the planet Venus.
It takes about 243 Earth days for Venus to rotate around on its
axis just once (which is what makes a day). And it takes 225
Earth days for Venus to follow its orbit all the way around the
sun (which is what makes a year).

A liwuli is a form of poem from Asia. Find out more on page 95.

Saturdays at the Imaginarium

Monday, my father
is nose-deep in newspapers.
Flick-flick…. *What!*
Flick-flick… *Jeez Louise!*
This world's gone crazy –
all money-money-money.
All me-me-me.

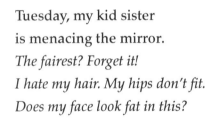

Tuesday, my kid sister
is menacing the mirror.
The fairest? Forget it!
I hate my hair. My hips don't fit.
Does my face look fat in this?

Wednesday, my brother
is bug-eyed on screen time.
Swipe-swipe / scroll. Click-click / like.
Can't talk ATM. (LOL). BRB.
J4F, GAL! GTG. PM-me.

Thursday, my mother's mojo
is running lo-lo.
Feed the laundry, iron the cat,
dinner the meeting, chair at eight,
drop off the bills, pay the kids –
hang on, wait!

Friday, I see our problem all too clearly.
Too. Much. Reality.
Happily, it's almost

Saturday –
cue the family chorus:
time to regroup, guys
and off we all troop
to the Imaginarium.

Here, the secret to success
is to choose
most astutely
how we mobilise
our minds…

Father, first up, fixes his focus
on a prime minister who listens
and within minutes, there she is
all ears and smiles and genuine interest.

Little sis pictures
the crowd on its feet as she takes to the stage
in trainers and t-shirt and mud-splattered jeans
to win the first ever Nobel Prize
for Being Yourself and/or Scuffing Your Knees.

Each week, my bro conjures up
the same trio of solid friends
and these real amigos talk and laugh and share and spill
till their hearts and guts are hanging out
like untamed shirt tails.

My mother is more inventive
than the rest of them put together.
Today she fills her mind with a phoenix
and takes to the sky, circling the sun for a hundred years
till eventually, spent, she bursts into flames
to be reborn again. And again. And again.

Meanwhile I've slipped into a secret side room,
locked the door
and imagined
the Imaginarium.
(Well, who did you think
runs this whole show!)

And then the clock calls time
and home we go, the five of us
arm in arm and grinning like idiots –
a family so full of bright ideas
so primed with potential
so souped up with hopes and dreams
and the means to realise them

that come Sunday,
absolutely anything
could happen.

And Now for the Weather
in Wonderland

Today will be a pool of tears, with prolonged spells of *who stole the tarts*?

During the early morning there may be scattered saucepans, but these should disperse like half no-time, and by lunch the air will taste of shrinking directly.

In the afternoon we may see a light shower of long, sad tails with possible outbursts of pig and pepper, followed later by uncomfortable conditions for flamingos who prefer the left side of the mushroom.

The evening will bring several strong blasts on the trumpet, after which the sky will seem much more *silence in court!* – particularly for those wearing little more than a pack of cards and some mischief.

By nightfall, expect the onset of girls shutting up like telescopes.

Tomorrow will either be much the same or completely different, and then for the weekend – an ear-to-ear grin nearly two miles high, with a low trembling voice rising to a perfect scream.

Poem by a Polite Rebel

I'm diving up the downpipe.
I'm blowing my own bubble.
I'm standing out from every crowd
        (if that's not too much trouble?).

I'm grooving to my inner tune.
I'm doing what I do.
When you say right, I'll hang a left
        (if that's okay with you?).

I'm questioning the answers.
Unearthing my own finds.
I'm overwriting history
        (that is, if no-one minds?).

Getting Real

Picture this:
you don't believe in wings.

In your world
planes never took off.

Birds drop like bombs from trees
and brood over internal injuries.

Butterflies
are your unicorns.

At night
you dream of marching.

The Circus Boy Gets a Funny Feeling

Something's amiss in the big top tonight.
The lions are restless. The tiger's eyes burn.
The ring hints at danger… a glare in the lights?

The horses are skittish. The dogs' barks have bite.
The acrobats tumble at every turn.
Something feels odd in the big top tonight.

The elephants rumble. The parrots take flight.
The clowns have stopped laughing, their faces look stern.
They've sensed the ring's danger. What stares through
    the lights?

Trish on the tightrope looks far from tight
and the juggler's dropped seven balls and an urn.
Something's off course in the big top tonight.

Trapezes and bungees are losing height.
The fire-eater's choking, it's more than heartburn.
The ring's tinged with danger. Risk flares in the lights.

You might think me foolish, too quick to take fright
but I'm begging you, friends, please heed my concern.
Something feels wrong in the big top tonight –
some danger awaits us. What lurks
    in those lights?

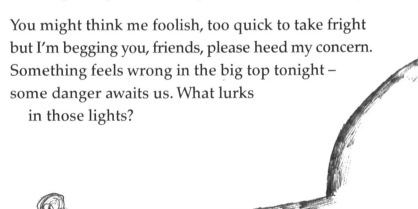

Dark, My Friend

Darkness came
and wrapped
its gentle arms
around me,

smoothed away
the worry lines
that marred my brow,

soothed away
the great and smaller
troubles
of the day.

Dark, my friend,
I'm feeling
lighter now.

My Grandma's a Straight-Talking Woman

And she knows what's not, where's there
and a thing or who, like never to speak of cold soup
and that each mango has its moment.

The best time to plant a spoon, she tells me
was seven bends ago. And speaking of time
she's well aware that she has Wednesdays
but sees no good in standing around looking like September.

When I come to her with a problem, she whispers
'Rubber ducks work wonders, but one white cloud
can shift into two brown cows on a sixpence.'

Sometimes she'll scold me
for messing with thought expellers
or walking with my elbows.
'Nothing worse,' she says, 'than a door-hinge gobbler
or one who counts stars
while others put a candle to it'.

She remembers the days when snakes wore vests
and dogs were tied with sausages.

'Did I tell you about the time,' she sighs
'when your grandad gave me ravens?
I was quite the biscuit back then
and he was a real piece of the moon.'

I ask her, 'When will I see the world
the way you do, Grandma?'

She laughs and says
'When the shark sings on the mountain.
When frogs grow hair.
On the day the fireman get paid
and when you let a little spark
go a very long way.'

Dancing with Life

I beckoned to the floor
missed buses and lost races.
We body-popped till sore.

I held out my hand
to every failed exam.
We lindy-hopped. We can-canned.

I slipped my arm around the waist
of *Chicken! Loser! Nerd!*
We skip-jived at a pace.

I chose the longest, dullest week
and pressed it to my chest
as we cha-cha'd cheek to cheek.

I tipped and doffed my hat
to a hundred horrid haircuts.
We mambo'd, tango'd, tapped.

Feeling bold, I turned to face
my darkest, rawest faults.
I took them in my arms, we bowed
and broke into a waltz.

From What Is to What If

It's not as hard as most folks fear
to journey over there from here.

From stuck-in-the-mud
to poised-on-the-brink –

it's *precisely* as far
as we think.

Cookin' Up a Universe

Particle soup!
Particle soup!
Start with a big pot
of particle soup –

add in some photons, a few cosmic strings
and out pops a jungle and six chicken wings.

Mix in some quarks and a mini black hole
which may create rain clouds or loud rock 'n' roll.

Chuck in some bosons: one X and a Higgs.
Result? Iron ore and a kilo of figs.

Stir in a lepton, a handful of WIMPs,
then watch as the room fills with glassware and shrimps.

Three light neutrinos, a muon or two
will often as not yield a tree kangaroo.

Gravitons, gluons and monopoles (four)
will either make peas or a long civil war.

Choose your ingredients, roll out the dice
and pray that the world you've just made will taste nice.

Particle soup!
Particle soup!
Boil up a big pot
of particle soup.

All the Thoughts
That've Ever Been Thunk

What if
the air was thick
with all the thoughts
that've ever been thunk
and all the thoughts
that've yet to be thinked?

Imagine them
in their billions and trillions
buzzing about on the breeze
like a cross between clouds and music and mosquitoes –

thoughts about how to play high F on saxophone
without squeaking

thoughts about who to tell about your day
when no-one in your family is speaking

thoughts about how to get from Bristol to Crewe
before there were bikes or cars or trains or planes

thoughts about how to peel a banana
when your left hand is missing or busy or sprained

thoughts about why people do mean things
and why dogs have tails and how gravity works

thoughts about doing several truly mean things
to Clarissa-flipping-Ibsen when she sneers and smirks

thoughts about inventing the light bulb and the wheel
and a way of not feeling cold when you're wet

thoughts about that joke that Maddox told
and I didn't really get

and what if
my brain was a radio –
half transmitter, half receiver
fizzing with all these flying thoughts
as they whizzed across the airwaves
from there to here, from here to there

and what if I learnt
to fine-tune my radio
so it picked up and played
only the thoughts I like the best –

funny little thoughts, like
what if the air was thick
with all the thoughts
that've ever been thunk.

PS. Just in case you're curious, 'thunk' and 'thinked' aren't real
words (unless of course you tune your radio to thynk they are).

Questions on an Empty Stomach

When's lunch?
What's for lunch?

If I eat lunch at four
will it still be lunch?

When I say lunch, you say dinner.
Who's right? When's tea?

Why does broccoli taste broccoly
and custard custardy?

If I pretend to like tomatoes
will they feel delighted or deceived?

How did all these things on my plate
get here?

Does lunch that's come a long way
taste tired?

Do fish from laughing rivers
go down better than glum ones?

Why doesn't everyone
have enough to eat?

And would it help if I skipped lunch
and just stayed here asking questions?

I Is for Empathy

I see Randall standing, awkward and alone, by the wall.
I see Jazmin's eyes bloodshot red. She's been crying again.
I see the bruise that Brian tries to hide behind a hat.

Can I imagine a whole year without a single friend?
Can I imagine losing my Dad, then leaving my country?
Can I imagine never feeling safe in my own home?

I feel my shoulders hunch, my stomach churn.
I feel my blood burning, my head swimming.
I feel my jaw clench, my throat tighten.

I feel my heart's chill.
And then, I feel my heart's warmth.

Connie in the Spotlight

Connie
can you sing us all a song?
                No, I can't.

Connie
can you show us if you're strong?
                No, I can't.

Connie
can you do a little dance?
                No, I can't.

Connie
can you spell the word 'perchance'?
                No, I can't.

Connie
can you count how much you've grown?
                No, I can't.

Connie
can you blow on this trombone?
                No, I can't.

Connie
can't you manage just one tune?
                No, I can't.

Connie
can you eat what's on this spoon?
                No, I can't.

For pity's sake Connie
can you do something, please!
I can keeping saying no
till you leave me in peace.

No Such Thing

There's no such thing
as moonlight, they say.
But –

I've bathed in it, played in it
stayed up too late in it

walked with it, stalked it
and talked girl-to-orb with it

danced till I'm numb in it
stuck out my tongue at it

jumped over cows with it
made secret vows to it

tickled white fish in it
whispered a wish to it

munched midnight snacks in it
practised wise-cracks with it

drifted to sleep in it
knelt down to weep in it

hugged the cool breeze
splashed in warm seas
leapt high as fleas
and scuffed both my knees in it.

No such thing as moonlight?
Please!

*Technically there's
no such thing as
moonlight. It's really a
reflection of the sun's
light on the moon's
surface. Or so they say.*

What the Magician Whispered

Give me
    HOORAY!
    BRAVO!
    ENCORE!

and I'll give you
    one wish, every day
    always *yes*, never *no*
    open on your every door.

Give me
    BOO!
    HISS!
    LAME!

and I'll give you
    full bladder / no loo
    a cobra's fatal kiss
    last place in every game.

Give me
    two white rabbits from one black cat
    an ace of hearts from a jack of spades
    doves released from a locked-tight cage

and I'll give you
    my hat
    my cape
    the stage.

Spell for the Boy Who Kissed and Told

May all the world's dogs dine
on the homework you strived over.

Let your bedclothes turn carnivorous
and your pillows grow thistles.

May the landscape of your face break out
in boils, blisters, warts and zits

while roundworms, leeches, catfish, toads
ooze – in your shoes.

Let your bike strike up a fight with a brick wall
and your next haircut smack of a car crash.

May every mention of the word *trust*
bring you out in hiccups

and your mother's tongue know just one word –
no.

Let the wind whip up and strip you down
to knickers – frilly, pink (your sister's).

And, stuck for luck, I pray you never stumble
on a horseshoe, rainbow, rabbit's foot

but tumble into quicksand, tar, a flood.
May those lips be sealed for good.

No / Can / Do

I can't
for the life of me
fathom this sum

can't
for the spoon and the fork
and the knife of me
see how it's done

can't
for the foot in the mouth
and the teeth on the tongue
and the head in my hands of me
understand

can't
for the wasp in my hair
and the faraway stare
and the halt, who goes there
and the stop, don't you dare of me

can't
for the sir it's not fair
and the send up a flare
and the please say a prayer
and the nowt to declare
'bout the root of the square
and the what do I care of me

can't
        for the
        oh –
        hang on…

I can!

Eight, Maybe Nine, Magicians You Never Knew About

There's a grey-haired man who sits all day at the station
but never once gets on a train. He's a magician.

That kid at the swimming pool
with four orange armbands and a red rubber ring –
the one who's covered in rashes again. Also a magician.

Have you seen the woman with the blue headscarf and
    the half-smile
selling The Big Issue outside Victoria Park? She's a magician.

The Prime Minsters of New Zealand, Iceland and Denmark
are all magicians.

That dude on the news who's been arrested again
for chaining himself to a tree, he's some kind of magician.

Mr Oliver, my best-ever genius teacher
says at my age, all his school marks were D.
Do you suppose he might be a magician?

There's this waitress in the café where my Dad sometimes
    takes me.
While we eat egg and chips, she washes the dishes
and stares out of the window. I think she's a magician.

Yesterday our crazy old neighbour Diego went ballistic
when I lobbed my ball right into his roses.
No worries though, since deep down I know
that guy's definitely a magician.

One night he told me
that if, when I close my eyes
I can remember the taste of the last orange I ate
or find a way to feel warm inside on a chill day
or imagine myself in any other time, place, mood or skin
than the one I'm in
then I, too,
could well be a magician.

Three Wondering Haikus

Before gravity
was discovered, did we all
take things more lightly?

How can the past be
history when we're talking
about it right now?

Since the world is round
is the furthest place from here
also the nearest?

No Unauthorised Vehicles
(poem for a sign on a gate)

Then authorise my vehicle.
So rubber-stamp my car.

I'm done with steering oh-so-near
I long to journey far

but every time I venture out
I'm halted by a sign –

Keep Out! Be Gone! Just Go Away!
This Road is Mine, All Mine!

Dear sirs, it's you who've made this
the road where I must go

with all your tempting notices,
the ones that tell me: *No.*

Wild Child

Child, were you born in a field?
Yes, and then brought up by bears.
And yes, that is mud on my feet.
And yes, that's a nest in my hair.

So when you say –
come inside, child
shut the door
draw the blinds

I say
  no.
    No!
      No.

For sure, I have rocks in my head.
And yes, when I cry there's a flood.
And yes, half my mind's in the sky
and the sea makes its waves in my blood.

So when you say –
be quiet, child
put some shoes on
sit still, will you

I say
  no.
    No!
      No.

Watching the Adverts on TV

We're beautiful, you're ugly.
We're rich, you're stony broke.
We're popular, you're lonely.
We're laughing, you're a joke.

Our bikes are new, yours rusty.
Our houses big, yours small.
Our boots have won 'Best Boot' awards,
yours couldn't kick a ball.

We understand your shortfalls.
But don't quit now. Aim high.
Come join us on the winning side –
go shopping. Buy, buy, buy!

It's Sort of Like

Do you ever wonder
if you're a hamburger child
in a fish finger family?

A string bean
in a mushy peas world?

I said this
to my big brother
and he said,

'Sis, you're a slow train
to my high-flying fighter jet,'

and I said, 'Thanks bro,
for taking my metaphor
and mowing me down with it.
You big wet Monday morning.'

A Matter of [   ]

[Sub-Saharan Africa / Time / Wednesday] is a great healer.
I haven't got [underwear / surfaces / time].
It'll be different next [time / door / wardrobe].

It's about [three / a boy / time].
We're running out of [time / vacuums / musical instruments].
We have all the [car parks / time / ideas] in the world.

[Compost / time / the moon] is on our side.
There's a [time / field / weather] for everything.
This is my [fence / teddy bear / time].

What [time / river / drink] do you call this?
It's high [five / time / tide] you did something about the
    situation.
I've told you a hundred [lies / hairstyles / times].

I'd love to travel back in [trousers / time / custard].
I need more [time / tingle / test results].
Only [hosepipes / smiles / time] will tell.

Hands Off

Sometimes at night, I loosen my hands
and let them float free

to give them a break from their daily routine
of pointing, picking up, touching, waving

which leaves me and my wrist-ending arms in peace
to drift off to sleep, to dream of new worlds

where our hands are above us, circling like birds
or stretching like bridges to reach over rivers

and then we wake up, my arms, wrists and me
to see happy hands fetching fruit, toast and tea

and we want to say thank you, but find we can't talk.
Seems our mouth has popped out for a walk.

The Story of the Story

It was born in the breath of a tiger.
It stirred in the soul of a crow.
The whole thing kicked off with a six-legged snake.
This, for sure, I know.

It trickled from hills down to deserts.
It rolled out from jungle to moor.
It ripped through the air like a cyclone on skates.
Of this, at least, I'm sure.

It saved us from measles and demons.
It starved us / it kept us well fed.
It caused every war, every battle we've fought.
Or, that's what's always been said.

It's the truth. We must sit up and listen.
It's fake and invented. It's old.
Believe it or don't, but it lives in us all –
for this is the story we've told.

My Great Big Appetite
for Mystery

In the second-hand store
it wasn't the book's cover
that drew me to it.

It wasn't the blurb on the back
waxing on about the book's benefits
and teasing me with tasters
of what treats lay within.

Nor was it the perplexing message
a previous reader had penned in red ink
in the index (*if you find this, PLEASE HELP*)
followed by a foreign-looking phone number.

It honestly wasn't the hand-drawn map
on the blank page at the back
that looked a tad rough, as if scrawled in a rush
and seemed to be suggestive of treasure.

It wasn't even the coded notes *(m33t m1dn1ght)*
scribbled in multiple margins
or the dark stains *(wine? blood?)*
splattered across particular pages
as if to illustrate that this literature was linked
with something deliciously suspicious.

What it was, was this –
pressed between pages 62 and 63:
a perfect slice of peppered salami.

I whipped it out
and gulped it down
and tossed that boring old book in the bin.

Goldilocks' Little Sister Pops into the Careers Service

When I grow up
do you s'pose I could be

an open-door follower
        a boiled egg swallower
                a deep sleep wallower?

An empty house tormentor
        a flying toast inventor
                a dream-world presenter?

A front door deflator
        a doughnut motivator
                a slumber cultivator?

An open window scorer
        a cereal explorer
                a record-breaking snorer?

In short, something better
than miss goldi-head
who somehow got famous
for break-in / breakfast / bed.

Centuries of Questionable Kings

Did Pippin the Middle long to make it to the top?
Did Ivar the Boneless have a tendency to flop?
Was Stephen the Precious almost always in a strop
and did Ferdinand the Bomb ever drop?

Did Louis the Popular have lots of Facebook friends?
Was Haakon the Crazy absolutely round the bend?
Did Piero the Unfortunate sustain a sticky end
and Llywelyn the Luxurious just spend?

Was Edward the Eloquent ever lost for words?
Did Domnall the Speckled get mistaken for a bird?
Did Vasily the Cross-Eyed see the world as mostly blurred
and was William the Silent ever heard?

Was Louis the Unavoidable glued to your side?
Did Alfonso the Candid despair of those who lied?
Was Olaf the Titbit raw or sautéed, baked or fried
and was James the Rash just itching to be tied?

Was Harold the Bluetooth the world's first wireless king?
Did Haakon the Broad-Shouldered tend to take things on
    the chin?
Was Ferdinand the Fickle up and down, then out, then in
and did Louis the Debonair wear bling?

Was Brochwel the Fanged known to bark and then to bite?
Did Frederick the Bitten cross his path one fateful night?
Did Constantius the Pale turn a pasty shade of white
and Garcia the Trembler get a fright?

Did Alfonso the Slobberer give anything but drool?
Was Childeric the Idiot a mug, a chump, a fool?
Was Bolko the Strict uber-stern and super-cruel?
And were any of them really fit to rule?

Believe it or not, this poem is based on 27 true stories. These are the
nicknames of 27 real historical royals, monarchs and nobles.

A Word of Advice, Sunshine

Keep the sun in your pocket
for grey winter days.

If a door slams, don't knock it –
put the sun in your pocket
and be on your way.

Cut the heart loose, don't lock it
but keep the sun in your pocket.

There'll be grey winter days.

Important Instructions

1. How to disappea

Shauna Darling Robertson

grew up in Northumberland, spent many years as a Londoner and now lives in Somerset. She's had lots of different jobs over the years – librarian, chef, web editor, charity trustee, travel agent and more. Her poems for adults and children are widely published in magazines and anthologies and have won, or been shortlisted for, a number of awards. They've also been performed by actors, displayed on buses, used as song lyrics, turned into short films and repurposed as comic art. Shauna says, 'I love working with other writers, artists, musicians and performers to explore all kinds of different ways of making and sharing poetry.'

Saturdays at the Imaginarium is her first children's book.

Find out more at **www.shaunadarlingrobertson.com**

Jude Wisdom

studied visual communication at Corsham Art College, where everyone rode around on bikes in rural bliss. Entering the real world, she illustrated for magazines and followed this by writing and illustrating children's books, namely *Whatever Wanda Wanted*, *Miss Chicken and the Hungry Neighbour* and *Billy Jupiter*, and illustrated *Go to Bed Doodlehead* for author Ian Whybrow. Jude lives in Bath and draws her inspiration from time spent in her local bookshop café, where her creative ideas come to life and where she sketches in her precious notebooks while meeting lots of new people and talking to the booksellers.

Her latest picture book, *The Island*, is published by Troika.

A quick chat with Shauna and Jude

Shauna, when did you start writing poems? What's the first poem you remember writing?

When I was around 6 or 7 I think. I remember writing one about ghosts and monsters flying around my bed. Sometimes it took me ages to get to sleep and I'd lie there in the dark imagining all sorts of things.

Why do you write poetry?

I like the way poetry leaves room for lots of different ways of thinking and feeling, and diverse ways of understanding and experiencing things. I love its rhythm and sound (like music) and the way it creates strong images in the mind. Also, poetry's compact so it challenges you to work hard to find specific ways of saying what you want to say.

Jude, what's your favourite poem in the book?

I love them all! Shauna's poems are great to work with because they're so rich with imagery, but at the same time they also leave lots of room for interpretation. I'm particularly fond of 'Wild Child', which was the first one I illustrated. 'The Story of the Story' is wonderful too, it conjures up so many pictures in my mind.

Shauna, what's your favourite illustration?

That's a tough one, I love them all too! I really like the curiosity of the girl in 'Open Wide'. The poem is an invitation to open our minds as well as our mouths, and the illustration captures that perfectly. And I have a soft spot for 'Wild Child' too. There's a bit of that child in me.

How did you work together on the book? What was it like?

It was lots of fun. We had quite a few meetings along with the book's editor, Roy Johnson, to discuss ideas, look at sketches, drink tea and eat cake. Some of our meetings were quite long because we'd end up talking and laughing about all kinds of other things too.

Jude, what do you most like to draw?
Until recently, it was lions. Now I think it's wolves. For a while my wolves were rubbish and looked a bit like warthogs, but I reckon I'm getting better at them.

Shauna, is poetry good for the imagination?
For sure! Good poetry has a kind of magical quality, whether we're reading it, writing it or performing it. It focuses our full attention on something: a thought, a feeling, an event or a moment. That kind of attention changes how we look at things and how we experience them. Every poem I write or read or hear gives me new ideas.

Jude, what would you do if you weren't an artist?
I'd be an opera singer.

What are you both working on next, after this?
Jude: Right now I'm illustrating a wonderful song written by a friend. Later I'm planning an exhibition of artwork based on a novel by another friend (I have some very clever friends!). And my picture book, *The Island*, is coming out soon so I'll be doing events and activities around that.
Shauna: I'm working on my next poetry book, with support from Arts Council England. It's all about mental and emotional health and wellbeing. After that I'd love to work on a picture book too (I have a couple of ideas up my sleeve but I'm not sure if they're any good!).

On the web

Visit Shauna's website
www.shaunadarlingrobertson.com
where you can find some Imaginarium extras.

There are videos. There are poetry films. There are voice recordings of Shauna reading some of her poems. There's a few sneaky peaks behind the scenes into the making of the Imaginarium. And there's a blog with prompts for using your imagination to look at things and think about things a little bit differently, with ideas for creating your own poems and artwork.

What's a liwuli?

Remember the liwuli from page 37? A liwuli is a form of poem from Asia. Here's how it works:

1. It has three verses.
2. The first verse must have 31 syllables and be a set of instructions, written all as one line with no line breaks.
3. The second verse has 14 syllables, broken into 3 lines. You can have any number of syllables per line, as long as they total 14.
4. The third verse must have 10 syllables broken into 2 lines (again with any number of syllables per line), and this verse must be a question or questions.

It's easier than it sounds (honestly) – go on, have a go!

Thanks

Shauna would like to say a big thank you, merci, muchas gracias and obrigada to The Caterpillar magazine and to Bloomsbury, Macmillan, Otter-Barry Books, poetryroundabout.com and bethechangekids.org, who first published some of the poems you've just read here (or, if you're reading this book backwards, some of the poems you're about to read here).

Many thanks to Rachel Rooney and Roger Stevens for their support and encouragement, without which these poems would probably still be loitering in Shauna's imagination (which isn't a bad place to loiter, but a book's a good place too).

To Jude Wisdom, for her wonderful artwork and for being a blast to get to know and hang out with while we were working on this book, a special thank you. And a great big, super-sized, don't-hold-back-on-the-fries thank you to Roy Johnson, Martin West and Louise Millar at Troika.

Last but not least, a thousand thanks to Dave Denyer for giving me the time and space to imagine and to write.